Confront The Shadows

A Poetic Quest

by

Following Whispers

Chapter and Verse Publishing

Copyright © 2019 Clinton Burns

First published in 2019 by
Chapter and Verse Publishing

All Rights Reserved. No part of this book may be reproduced in any format, print or electronic, without explicit permission in writing from the copyright owner.

ISBN 978-1-9164627-1-7

To find out more about the author, this publication or their other available offerings, please go to:
followingwhispers.com

<u>Dedication</u>

This book of poetry is dedicated to my best friend in the entire Universe, Luke Ruddock. You've always been there through thick and thin, never judging, super supportive, and always able to make me smile. Not to mention being one of the most beautiful souls, anyone could dream of knowing. Thank you for showing me what a real friend is, and for actively making my life so memorable and amazing.

Contents

Introduction: The Path Less Travelled	1
Checkpoint	4
Consensual Paralysis	8
Love Cycle	11
Fear To Love	16
4 Seasons Of Loneliness	19
About Time	22
Black-I-Hole	25
"Spoken" (Thought) Pt. 1 - Redemption	27
"Spoken" (Thought) Pt. 2 - Twisted	30
Life... Spent!	33
Heroless: (1) Tragic	35
Heroless: (2) Feeding The Furnace	39
Heroless: (3) Repairing A Sinking Ship	43
Heroless: (4) Hiroshima Times	47
Heroless: (5) Non-Organic Produce	53
Pollen	57
Rusty Cogs	60
Exile Of A Scribbled Angel	62
Humble Crumble	64
Adiós!	67
Forever Love	69

Pot Luck	71
Empathy	72
Blessed	74
Meat The Muncher	76
Killing My Buzz	79
The Difference	82
I Knows It, I Grows It	85
The Age Of Plenty	88
Dearly Departed	89
About The Author	92

The Path Less Travelled

Hello, and welcome to my continued quest for personal growth. This is my second collection of published poetry (the first being "Proceed With Awesome"), written to give the proper and due respect to my personal milestones and life-affirming moments, but also to speak to you. I want to show you that all of our lives have tough challenges and obstacles, and rewarding times too; that you are not alone in feeling alone; that somebody cares and wants to help you find your way to some place better, and that we can get there quicker together.

I have always been a dab hand at solving problems, generally with whatever I had in close proximity to me. I swiftly became an 'Agony Uncle' to many of my friends and family, colleagues and the like. I've always enjoyed helping others and creating better realities for them, but a person's physical reach can only span so far, for most, this is limited to a few cities, or a region at most.

One of the great things about writing, is that it can travel across national borders and continents, with no need for a visa application, it can move faster than any wildfire and create an amazing amount of positive change in the World, something I've witnessed first-hand.

Life has really thrown me some curve balls over the years, (many of which feature in "Proceed With Awesome"), testing my resolve, and yet here I stand, more positive than I have ever been, more determined to do good in this World, for the benefit of all. I feel that facing and overcoming these dark trials and tribulations, has made me a better, stronger person, something I hope and believe all of you can and will achieve, if you haven't already.

I'm by no means perfect, nobody is, but I feel we can all do more with and get a lot more from this gift of life we've been blessed with. In order for that to occur, we first need to walk the path less travelled, by facing our demons; facing our fears; facing our oppressors; and challenging them all, eventually removing the power they have over us. So while most of the poetry in this book has a seemingly dark feel to it, it's brimming with good intentions, ultimately, to enable us to build a brighter future for ourselves and others.

For that to be possible though, we have to take a long hard (metaphorical) look in the mirror first, confronting the shadows we find in the process. Its a journey of discovery, but fortunately, you don't have to go it alone, we can head there together, so what are we waiting for, let's get to it!

Confront The Shadows: A Poetic Quest

Checkpoint

I'm set in position, confident and keen,
"Attention all drivers, start your engines please!"
Ignition, rev, rev, keeping the needle between,
Then I put my foot down as the lights turn green.

My wheels spin and the gravel underneath them sprays,
This course has been constructed to determine our place,
In the ranking, it seems real, but it's a virtual race,
Like the racing simulators in many an arcade.

It costs a lot more, it can be very expensive,
So everyone means Business, it's very competitive,
We have to do several laps, thus it's kinda repetitive,
Every action counts, only losers are negligent.

You have to prove you're better than average, or else,
No big trophy or plaque will be sitting on your shelf,
No medal or winner's bubbly, just limited wealth,
So you're not supposed to put others before self.

Confront The Shadows: A Poetic Quest

Unless they're on your team and need this more than you,
Or they supply your lifestyle, thus nothing you can do,
Now you're familiar with the culture and obligations too,
Let's get back to the race and see how I do.

I come up to the 1ˢᵗ turn, it's a medium right,
Lay off the gas a bit and steer quite tight,
Then punch on the accelerator, manoeuvring so nice,
Overtaking 2 vehicles on the inside.

Such a swift action, by the time they discover,
I'm out of here, it's too late, and I'm after another,
I came up beside them, they forced me into the rubble,
Crashing into my bumper, "now they're asking for trouble"!

But it's not over, I swerve, but I get back on track,
The 2 that I took earlier are trying to get past,
So I do a little shimmy, they've got no chance,
I use my Burnout and overtake the next one's ass.

Confront The Shadows: A Poetic Quest

I go through a checkpoint and my time-limit increases,
If you don't make it, your time's up and no statistics,
Don't cross the line in time and you will be dismissed,
Although the driver behind me wasn't, I couldn't believe it!

Lucky for them, time ran out, but they still rolled over,
And received an extension, instead of facing Game Over,
It's cool though, no mirror check or glance over shoulder,
I've been preparing for this race, since last October.

I used my mushroom, after going over a question mark,
As I remembered, questioning can be a rewarding art,
Yet after my great driving, focusing very hard,
I still had people ahead of me, so I followed my heart.

It said *"if you don't like the prospects, don't accept them,
You don't have to be down in the face, like Stimpy's friend,
What was the little fella's name? ...ah, that's it, Ren,
Use your resources wisely and you'll be a Champion again."*

I went out of my way to go over another question,
Got a lightning strike and used it without hesitation,
This had the effect of shrinking the competition,
I sped past them all, finally reaching the leading position.

It felt great, I always knew that I could do it,
It was just a matter of patience and the drive to pursue it,
Although it's too early to celebrate, I must keep it moving,
Remain enthusiastic, because there's still a chance of losing.

But even then I'm still a Winner, I was born for this,
Everything's not riding on this race, which is fortunate,
So there's no room for disappointment or being morbid,
No matter what lies before me, I'm only moving forwards.

Test my resolve and you'll see, that I'm as solid as a rock,
Before my wheels fall off, I'll change them at the pit-stop,
I know for success, you have to give it all you've got,
And don't sell yourself short, when racing against the clock!

Consensual Paralysis

Back and forth, I'm tossing and turning,
I attempt to wake up, but it's just not working,
Trapped in a sleep state, and my muscles are hurting,
From fighting a force that's evil and unearthly.

They invaded our Planet, bent on destruction,
Murder, theft and alien reproduction,
The current perception is we cannot trust them,
So I've killed many of them and continue to bus' guns.

But wait a minute! Aren't they quite like us?!
Humans kill, steal and breed too, plus have rifles,
Someone's got this twisted, are they taking the Michael?
Showing this topping, without the rest of the trifle.

All we can say, is that we were here first,
Yet even that's flawed, as our true history's blurred,
For those in control, that's the way it's preferred,
They define sanity, yet they're the most disturbed.

So here I am, caught up in an intense dream,
That really seems ever so life-like to me,
Illustrating the sick and twisted mentality,
That many of us adopt, but few of us can perceive.

Having reached a conclusion without concluding the action,
I stopped the bullets in mid-air, like Neo had done,
Saw the Mindtrix' Code, it's no longer a distraction,
Became the Master of my own speed, strength and reactions.

I'd freed myself from illusions and suddenly awoke,
About time too! That prison was no joke!
Why haven't I heard of this happening to other folk?
Am I the only one or am I an isotope?

Escaping permanent atrophy and gasping for breath,
Feeling like I'd been revived from an almost certain death,
On my bed, exhausted, I turned on my TV set,
It's quite scary and ironic what I saw next...

A reporter in the Gulf giving exposure,
On British and other troops in Iraq causing explosions,
After causing problems, our leaders rebuke the commotion,
What do they expect from their hypocritical notion!

With no clear path or logic, how can you get through,
Troublesome times, dark skies, and find a better view?!
Killing more of your own, than an enemy will ever do,
Less concerned about peace, than about your hairdo.

Murdering, torturing and oppressing civilians,
Supplying Israel with the weapons to massacre Palestinians,
Double standards on Human Rights, Poverty, Immigration,
What awful morals, we are showing the children!

You expect us to sit back, complacent and always trusting,
While you feast on the Game, you even brought stuffing,
Pursuing selfish interventions, sanctions and bullying,
"People! Should we frown, believe their lies... or do something?!"

Love Cycle

I know I sometimes express my thoughts esoterically,
Although I strive to show them passionately and vivid,
Anyway, I realized something that I'd like you to see,
Parallels in my experiences of cycling and dating women.

I started both not long after I'd learned to walk,
A little boy, with a big afro and chubby cheeks,
Granted, my legs were weak and I couldn't smooth-talk,
But I was eager, even with my limited strength and speech.

My first bike was a tricycle, metallic, in red and yellow,
In shorts and vest, I'd peddle without a care in the World,
I also got close to females, by dancing or saying hello,
My 3 early fascinations, music, cycling and girls.

I had my first proper girlfriend at 5 years old,
She had the added bonus of being the girl next-door,
Plus in the same class at school, so we were quite bold,
Sneakily kissing under the table, by dropping pens on the floor.

Confront The Shadows: A Poetic Quest

I got my first two-wheeler bike about the same time,
I really needed steering practice, especially with corners,
I recall my 2 cousins pushing me 'round that Close of mine,
And when I couldn't turn or stop, I flew into a thorn bush.

That didn't stop me though, I got straight back on again,
Like when my girlfriend left, I continued searching for love,
Even though I'd lost my neighbour, kissing partner and friend,
I knew I'd find 'The One' someday, although I was young.

Fast forward a few years, I'm still at the same school,
Going out with a pretty girl, who lived in the next street,
She liked me, but acted shy, then made me feel a fool,
When she kissed another boy, instead of giving sugar to me.

Thus ending my first strong dose of infatuation,
We otherwise got on great, so it was such a pity,
That things didn't work out, as she couldn't be faithful,
Anyway, months later her Parents moved her to another city.

Then soon after something happened, which is really weird,
Because of a loose column on my bike's handlebars,
I had an accident, in the street where she once lived,
That was pretty serious, it left me breathless and scarred.

So I stepped up my maintenance and stepped up my game,
This would guarantee no more injuries, or so I thought,
I wish I could've been right, I mean, what a shame,
I had to suffer more injuries than in full-contact sport.

At one point my cycling accidents always fell on a Sunday,
For various reasons, but it almost felt like a curse,
The flesh wounds were deep, the rest is hard to convey,
But what I can say, is the wounds to my heart were even worse.

Puncture kits were sometimes useful, but only occasionally,
If my tyres burst, I used my hand pump and a rubber patch,
If it still gave me trouble, I'd change the inner-tube totally,
As after a few repairs, it was likely to continue to go flat.

Confront The Shadows: A Poetic Quest

I had one relationship that turned really unpleasant,
And an accident that broke both bones in my forearm,
But it's also why I'm ambidextrous and wiser at present,
See, turning negatives to positives is just part of my charm!

I seriously put some of these bikes through their paces,
Usually they were faulty, though sometimes I caused the damage,
Within months, most of them needed replacing,
But always within a year, thus no candidates for marriage.

Although there was that one Diamond that got away,
A gift, in good condition and fairly low-maintenance,
With off-road capability and a fabulous frame,
Stolen during our first experience in a new environment.

Not claimed on the insurance, but I really felt the loss,
I spent years after, looking for one that was similar,
Only to find I had less influence, than in a coin toss,
So I had one specially made, using desired criteria.

The resulting creation, has brought joy and future promise,
Attention to detail, patience and persistence have paid off,
I feel we respect each other, being affectionate and honest,
Plus I'd be happy to remain this way, until my organs stop.

So this goes out to my currently concealed future Wifey,
I'm confident we'll unite, even if not for years,
We are made for one another, and will go together nicely,
There's no-one on this Planet, that I'd rather cycle with.

Fear to Love

Hello there, howdy, how are you doing?
Are you happy with your life and what you're pursuing?
Lie back on the couch and count to 10,
Then say the first thing that comes into your head...

Hmmm, that's interesting, please, continue...
I believe you conceal much darkness within you,
Probably stemming from a troubled childhood,
Leading to you feeling frustrated and misunderstood.

And probably resenting those who seem to be happy,
If your life were a record, it'd be warped and crackly,
But you would probably add scratches, or snap it in two,
Rather than remaster it, repair or renew.

This is the adversity we need you to surmount,
And during our sessions, we shall learn about,
The things that make you angry and why,
What torments or upsets you and the reasons behind.

Confront The Shadows: A Poetic Quest

I want you to tell me of your first bad memory...
Some people hold emotional baggage for many centuries,
We could explore yours with regression in time,
But if you'd rather conscious exploration, that's fine...

Okay, no worries, there are other techniques,
We can use to locate the source of your grief,
What's been you opinion of your Parents to date?
...Sure, that's actually a common complaint.

It's not your fault, nor entirely theirs,
And you feel neglected, worthless and scared,
Of being alone or what people think of you,
Or change, but for better or worse, change is overdue.

Still, it's your creation, so which do you prefer?
A 'WELCOME' mat or sign saying 'DO NOT DISTURB!'
On it? The latter's negative, draining your energy,
You even fight with your friends, everyone's an enemy.

Being positive and open-minded is much better,
Than protecting your heart, by putting it in a shredder,
This creates an egotistical, shallow human being,
Or one losing touch with their spirit and inner-feelings.

They are very materialistic and frequently depressed,
Possessing little common sense, always tired or stressed,
The two share a common bond, like sister and brother,
Both consumed by fear in one form or another.

So do you fear to love or can you change fear to love?
Because fear brings hate, then anger and spilled blood,
Fear's the reason for negativity, suffering and wars,
So I want you to identify and eliminate its cause.

Unfortunately today's session must come to a close,
Completing my book's exercises are what I propose,
Here's a copy, it's called '4 Seasons of Loneliness',
Until our next appointment, take care, all the best!

4 Seasons of Loneliness

In this section I wish to summarise the main points,
Made throughout this book, flexibly like joints,
To assist you in defeating your fear and distress,
Inspire you and get you feeling back at your best.

Autumn: Is the first season to be developed,
Where things turn bad and you are under-zealous,
Underlying problems start bubbling to the surface,
You waste your opportunities, thinking it's not worth it.

You may become reclusive, constantly unmotivated,
And keep sh*t in, like you are constipated,
Next you probably think entertainment's your only friend,
With no reason to smile, in front of others you'll pretend.

Winter: This makes you feel rotten, cold and bitter,
Your frown becomes frozen, now a permanent fixture,
It appears your sense of humour has gone into hibernation,
And the odds are, you're overindulgent in masturbation.

Using alcohol and drugs as an escape in the short-term,
And/or retail therapy of extreme proportions,
Some will look for fights, simply to vent their anger,
Strangers and loved ones, get harsh words or backhanders.

Others adopt a victim mentality and in turn,
The vibes they transmit are received and return,
In the form of abuse, neglect and storm clouds,
What would've been unacceptable before's, now allowed.

What ensues are people taking you for an unpleasant ride,
Or intimidating you, you feel even worse inside,
With unjustified, disgustingly huge debts and addictions,
Your only hope now is setting yourself restrictions.

Plus you must stick to them and learn discipline,
In order to improve your life and your qualities within,
Remember, to solve a problem, first admit you have one,
And if you want to see better days, you have to be strong.

Spring: The weather's been harsh, but gradually changing,
Your actions are more productive, after much rearranging,
You start to reunite with your positive essence,
Keep in mind the lessons learnt, they're very precious...

Like dealing with your emotions, not covering them up;
Being thoughtful and generous, without spending much;
Cut up all your credit cards; pay off all your debts;
Make amends for negativity; rectify your key regrets.

Summer: The first thing you should do is smile,
Love, have fun, laugh, enjoy the sunshine,
The seeds you planted blossomed, it was worth the wait,
Inspiration can be yours, when you look for it or create.

Everyone's true potential can and should be realised,
Increasing your self-esteem, when properly utilized,
But if the sky turns grey and you see decay, stay calm,
Email me your concerns via counselling.com

About Time

Time, how much do we have left,
Collectively or individually? *"Look man, who cares!"*
"I care!" Looking back at the time I've consumed,
I wonder if I've put those years to good use.

Or have I been wasteful, squandering it?
Would I achieve no more, even if I'd more with which,
I could do stuff, or would I be efficient like recycling,
And furthermore, could I recycle time like lightning?

When a second has passed, there's no known resurrection,
But it can be used to reflect on many learnt lessons,
If you reminisce on spent time, you use future tick-tocks,
Living in the past, time goes faster like stolen stock.

But if memories are blocked, what's the point in your life!
Apart from chain reactions in the people you've inspired,
And the memories of others, that you helped to create,
Is our life just a movie in which we participate?

Confront The Shadows: A Poetic Quest

I'm not sure, my mind is racing at the concept,
That we're loose with time, with no idea of what's left,
For us and others, friends, family, lovers,
Do you spend most of it outside or under the covers?

Have you seen and experienced all that you want to?
Have you lots of unmet desires, yet don't know which to do?
Well, my advice to you, is get to it right away,
You may not have forever, but you can do things day by day.

Although I still believe it's good to plan for your future,
Or the future of those dependent on you, for sure,
With a security blanket and backup plans in your arsenal,
Longevity and security, part of the same parcel.

You dictate your own survival, your own existence,
But many trade their rights for the clock, with no resistance,
Well, one things for sure, I know that I haven't,
And strive for more than the ideals of a work-life balance.

Confront The Shadows: A Poetic Quest

I guess that's partly why I'm sitting here writing,
On the eve of another year on this Earth, frightening!
Yes, time flies, before long, I'll be thirty,
If my timeline continues, i.e. if I'm worthy.

So what lies beyond, neither mystic nor I,
Could have a stab and definitely hit the bulls-eye,
But the future's so bright, I think I'll wear shades,
And use my intuition to score as high as I can in this game.

We all have a time limit, hidden from view,
With varied expirations for me and for you,
We can only guess. Hey, I've a question you know,
Will I be a day, or a year older tomorrow?

Some would say both, although I'm unsure,
Throughout my time here, my intentions remain pure,
Although the jury's still out, when will they decide,
If I've made a good impact? ...I guess, all in good time!

Black<I>Hole

The tock-tick, tock-ticking of an anti-clockwise mind,
WHO gave it a wind, and set it in motion,
Is it a mistake or a creation of destruction?
Engineered to break down the very essence of existence,
Will it therefore destroy its creator or become it?
Who should interpret such a concept?
And how long do they have to do so,
Before the rewritable disc is erased,
And left without a trace?!

Make haste! And do the unthinkable,
The uninkble, shall be penned from a fountain of blue,
Then removed by a clear solution that's applicable,
"HELP, HELP, I'm Melting!" they scream,
As they're made to feel unwanted and despised,
Then like good lies, kept invisible,
Deception, or merely the correction of an inaccuracy or fault?
But who's fault?! Whose is, was or will it be?
Someone has to take the fall, the blame, claim ownership,
Of this supposed lost property.

Confront The Shadows: A Poetic Quest

If an eye's only view is a blind-spot, then the wind changes,
Is it blind? ...and if so, does it remain thus,
Or can its sight be restored?
To enable recognition of a disturbing reality,
Everybody drowning in a negative current,
Where safety precautions have little or no effect,
There are no emergency services or lifeguards to save the day.

It must be a full moon! How else can this be occurring?!
Everyone's blood boiling, with no pilot or ignition,
Feral instincts rising like corpses on riverbeds,
Implicitly prevalent, ever-present,
Just waiting to resurface and cause chaos!
Biding time, building momentum steadily,
Approaching undetected to the naked eye,
With a stealth-like motion, until... **BOOM!!!**
It's here now, here and all around, as far as the eye cannot see!
Does it span the entire Universe? ...or merely ...within me?

"Spoken" (Thought) Pt. 1 – Redemption

"**Chicken!**" (*There's no way that I'm doin' that!*)
Is what the other kids said and thought,
As Tom started to sweat and thought (*Crap!*
I don't want to, but I've got to, I hope I'm not caught!)

If I don't do this, they'll think I'm a wimp!)
His conscience wouldn't override, after a struggle,
He went in and ran back out the shop in a blink,
Chased by the shopkeeper, "***Boy, you're in big trouble!***"

(*Why do these little bleeders wanna steal from me?*
At this rate, they'll soon put me out of business,
They may laugh now, but soon they'll be sorry,
There'll be nowhere nearby to get sweets, crisps 'n' biscuits!)

Tom finally reunited with his 'so-called' friends,
And handed Mark the 2 litre bottle of Red Square,
"*Not bad, but why's it not stronger than 5 percent!*"
(*I'm gonna have fun manipulatin' him with my dares!*)

Before long, Mark had the whole posse doing his dirt,
Anything that his warped mind could imagine,
From theft to throwing bricks at Holy Trinity Church,
Underage sex, joyriding, wagging and happy-slapping.

Until the day Mark's Mum was rushed to A&E,
After being mugged and abused, by a gang of fools,
(Damn, I bet I'd have caused the same, eventually,
It's really horrible being in the victims shoes!)

His Mother was beaten so badly, he hardly recognised her,
"It's gonna be alright Mum!" He gave her a hug,
(I hope she pulls through! I mean, she's a fighter,
But that look in her eyes, it's like she wants to give up.)

On the way to his Dad's, he acted out in his head,
What he'd do and how he'd feel if he got some revenge,
He decided, *(I'd feel worse, even if they were dead,*
Plus I need to change my ways, I can't pretend...

That I've been much better than whoever did this!)
Unfortunately, his Mother died from internal bleeding,
He felt like removing his prior acceptance and forgiveness,
Yet he focused on the positives, to help with his grieving.

The Police had no strong leads, so who could he blame?!
Therefore, he kept his vow to pursue redemption,
Mark spoke to the posse, "*I think you should do the same!*"
But most of them, including Tom, remained in detention.

Causing all kinds of mayhem, in and out of school,
"*I had to lose something precious in order to mature,*
Whether it's easy or hard, your lesson's overdue,
The choice is yours!" (*I'm just showin' you the easy door!*)

"See, I've realised karma really does come back 'round,
So stop the madness, before it's too late, please trust this,
You can avoid suffering like mine, if your balance is found,
Before the scales topple nastily, give back to the goodness!"

"Spoken" (Thought) Pt. 2 – Twisted

"Hey, Daz!" Daz turns around, (*I recognise that voice!*)
"Oh my God, Joanne!" (*She's as beautiful as ever!*)
"Girl, you look fabulous!" (*Still my number 1 choice.*)
"Thanks, in school I simply focused on being clever,

But now I put a lot of effort into lookin' my best."
"Well, it's obvious you do, I bet you're still really smart!"
"I don't need to be now, I make good money with little stress!"
(*I don't care, you can still have the keys to my heart.*)

"So who are you here with, anyone I know?"
"Just some peeps from work, come, I'll introduce ya,
People, this is Daz." **"Hi Daz!"** *"Hello!"*
"Me 'n' him are goin' to dance!" (*So I can seduce ya!*)

(*Okay, she must be single, from the way she's touchin' me!*)
"You're a great Dancer!" (*Meaning he must be good in bed!*)
"I don't usually do this, but will you come home with me?"
(*Yeah, I usually go back to their place instead!*)

Darren thought (*It's pretty sudden, but she's a nice girl.*)
"Okay, sure! What time dya wanna leave?"
"Let me just get my jacket." (*And I'll rock your World!*)
"Hey you lot, us two are goin', see you next week!"

"My friend's 'round here somewhere, still on the blag,
He's so distracted, he won't even notice I'm gone!"
(*I'd be on my own, if I hadn't bumped into Joanne,
Still, it's funny that I'm the one leavin' with someone!*

Lucky me, I'm sure she'll show me love 'n' respect.*)
(*This should be fun, I just hope he doesn't get attached!
He's got a fit body, I can't wait to get him into bed!*)
"Nice place you've got here, it must'a set you back!"

"Quit the small talk... strip off 'n' join me!"
"Okay." (*I want to get closer to this angelic beauty.*)
"That was amazing ...you've sexually spoiled me!
So it's only right I please you some more, it's my duty!"

"You're so considerate." (Cupid, draw back your bow,
And hit her with your arrow, so she's mine for life!)
(That was a good fun, plus I'm gettin' some off Ben tomorrow!)
"You know, I'm really glad I chose to spend the night!

Dya wanna meet up tomorrow?" "Sorry, I've got a date!"
"Is this a one-night stand?!" (Is she loose or somethin'?)
"Yep!" (Exactly what we should've done, back in the day!)
"I hate commitment and being the victim of dumping!

Come on, lighten up, we had a good time didn't we!?"
(Damn, get with the programme and stop being so dumb!)
"Trust me, it wouldn't work, even if we did things differently!"
(I prefer men on demand) "Hey, at least you got some!"

(The old me would still be chuffed, that we made love,
I guess my expectations were high, I'm strange in her eyes,
But now, I can't help feelin' that I'm down on my luck!)
"Bye, it's been real!" (I guess anyone can change and surprise!)

Life... Spent!

Me, bloody hungry!
Need tummy money!
Be money hungry,
Feed grumbly tummy...

Eat, lovely, yummy,
Meat curry, pudding!
Becoming chubby,
Greed... mucky, ugly!

Me... money hungry,
She... wouldn't hug me,
She... doesn't love me,
He... doesn't trust me.

Peace should be coming!
Feel bloody crummy,
See nothing funny,
Becoming grumpy.

Need p*ssy, buddies!
"Please Money, hug me!?
Keep Grumpy company!?
Treat Sonny lovely!?"

Leaked runny money,
She... bluntly f*cked me!
Feed Hungry Money,
...Sleep duppy, Dummy!

Heroless: (1) Tragic Ends & Beginnings

Interest, awareness, concern and discipline,
These are the qualities Mary possessed within,
A 30 year old lady actively investing in her health,
When it came to her well-being, she didn't mess about.

After finishing her daily exercise routine,
She showered, drank some fruit juice and began cooking,
Sat down to a lovely vegan meal with vitamins galore,
Ate several spoonfuls, then heard a knock at the door.

Mary got up and opened the door, to her surprise,
Two police officers were standing on the other side,
She welcomed them in, they both displayed a frown,
One said he had bad news and suggested she sat down.

She said *"hurry up and tell me, not knowing is torture!"*
"There's been an accident, your Husband and Daughter,
They were fatally wounded… Madam, I'm truly sorry,
We need you to accompany us and I.D. the bodies."

Her swelling eyes gave way and she wailed in disbelief,
　She even pinched herself, in the hope it was a dream,
But the nightmare was real, her whole World had collapsed,
Couldn't deal with the emotions, so she hid behind a mask.

　At the first opportunity she gathered various drugs,
　Took them all together, clearly wishing to push her luck,
But the chosen lethal cocktail, failed in its desired effect,
It didn't finish her off, it simply left her feeling wrecked.

But that didn't stop her trying, she didn't want to go on,
　She'd lost the will to live, along with her loved ones,
　So the cocktails continued in ever-increasing doses,
She surrendered all control, like being in deep hypnosis.

It had been ages since she'd worked out or practised yoga,
　No longer health conscious, those concerns were over,
　Her friends tried to help, she loathed their meddling,
　　In an effort to escape, she started using heroin.

Mixed with water, it was heated and propelled into her vein,
   Within seconds, it was everywhere, including her brain,
     She felt euphoric, but also increasingly nauseas,
It could've been the smack, but intuition made her curious.

Mary feared it could be linked to her gaining a few pounds,
   It was, inside her grew the child of her late spouse,
     Shocked, she went cold-turkey to ensure it survived,
  She wouldn't forgive herself, if the last part of him died!

It was harder than she thought, so she went to Dr. Bowman,
Who referred her to a methadone maintenance programme,
   To limit the damage to the foetus, through the placenta,
  "I'll refer you to an excellent specialised treatment centre."

  At the centre they prescribed her 90 milligrams a day,
   Which seemed more addictive, she decided not to stay,
  (*There must be another way*), she thought in her head,
    She mixed heroin with powdered milk and smoked it instead.

(*Smoking it's not so bad!*), She found out this was b*llocks,
  As the Doctor piled a guilt trip on her in huge dollops,
    "*You should've stayed in the treatment centre Mary,*
  The problems, which you will add to now, are very scary.

Complications with the pregnancy are now even more likely,
A tiny chance of none, but a greater chance there might be,
You're playing a dangerous game, they'll be born an addict,
  Any illness you catch, chances are they'll have it.

Not to mention genetic anomalies, tremors, constant crying,
  Jitters and a higher probability of your baby dying,
   I will also have to refer you to Social Services,
And they will decide if you display parental worthiness."

She looked inside herself musing (*there's no hero in 'ere,*
Only heroin 'ere, ruinin' mine and a life approaching near,
  I don't deserve this child or the gift of giving birth,
  So I vow, its first day, will be my last upon this Earth!)

Heroless: (2) Feeding The Furnace

Tony lay in the bath and stared at the ceiling,
Trying to make sense of his life and desolate feelings,
(Look at all the pain I've suffered in 36 years,
The torment of 20 lifetimes compressed in my tears)!

<Knock, knock> *"Anthony, do you need me to assist?"*
"No Mum, I'm fine! I'll be out in a bit!"
(*God, she's more persistent than an incurable disease,
I wish she'd get lost and let me rest in peace!*

*She's the main reason I'm screwed up, the silly bitch!
She verbally and emotionally abused me as a kid,
And now she wants to play Samaritan, I don't buy it,
I'll always see the monster inside, she'll never hide it!*)

His toes felt a bit cold, so he splashed them about,
He felt the sensation, but didn't hear the sound,
As Tony looked down the other end of the bath,
He saw 2 stumps, and the memories came flooding back...

Confront The Shadows: A Poetic Quest

(The Doctor said I'd occasionally forget some things,
And experience what they call 'Phantom Limbs',
I'm unhappy with everything and can't pretend at all,
My actions and mind-state of late are undefendable!

I started off binge drinking and smoking mad chronic,
But became confused, anxious, selfish, demonic,
Due to not being able to deal with my buried emotions,
Concerning my crap childhood, Mum's lack of devotion.

Even though the drugs worsened things in retrospect,
They had a hold on me, I loved gettin' wrecked,
They made me feel confident, helped me get fucked,
Made me feel free, when I was anything but!

It wasn't long before I yearned for something more,
So many other drugs, I almost sampled them all,
That was until Jeff introduced me to his friend Charlie,
Those first few lines at his engagement party...

Confront The Shadows: A Poetic Quest

Were most definitely in a league of their own,
It had my full attention, body-mind-blown!
I couldn't stop... I wanted the buzz 24/7,
To get more, I'd've scooped my brains out like melon.

I sold all my stuff, even my signed Pac CD,
And when I had no possessions left, I started thieving,
From neighbours, friends, even my own family,
When I got the chance to deal, I took it, gladly.

Not to pay the bills, that wasn't on my mind,
To buy some Pony or get high on my own supply,
Yeah, that's when I became really careless and greedy,
Sniffed a load of gear in my car, while I was speeding.

I was too busy in the mirror, powdering my nose,
That I didn't see the guy and girl try'na cross the road,
I thought I imagined them, soon after I was sorry,
It's ironic that I crashed into a Coca Cola lorry.

Confront The Shadows: A Poetic Quest

That's when I trapped my legs, they had to amputate,
But those two lost their lives, that's not a fair exchange!
Why should they pay for my reckless behaviour?!
The World should rise up and show its indignation!

On top of that, I've got my Mum giving me stress,
Becoming even more annoying in her intrusiveness,
Try'na play happy families, something we've never been),
"Anthony, that film you like is on the T.V!"

(I'm a f*ckin' grown man and she won't leave me alone,
Since the crash, she's practically taken over my home,
I've told her to p*ss off, but she doesn't pay attention,
She says she wants to make amends, achieve redemption.

I've got to leave this place, so I've made a 'Speedball',
A mix of Coke 'n' Heroin that's extremely lethal,
To escape my suffering, this price I pay is a pittance,
Au revoir, ta-ta, goodbye and good riddance!!!)

Heroless: (3) Repairing a Sinking Ship

"Good Afternoon everyone, thank you for coming,
Here you can be open, without feeling we're judging,
I see lots of new faces, please don't be shy,
Tell us your name, compulsion and the reasons behind."

"Hi, my name's Christina, I was a compulsive helper,
For so long, my feelings remained under shelter,
Well, locked in a cage or in air-tight compression,
I was bubbly externally, yet filled with depression.

Harbouring secrets of an unpleasant past,
In order to ignore them, I'd always come last,
In my priorities, I didn't see myself as important,
When I only helped others, my own pain was dormant.

This way the hurt didn't increase, yet it didn't go away,
I never confronted it, which left the burden here to stay,
And I continued interfering, controlling, restructuring,
But like a dictator, I mostly added to the suffering!

Confront The Shadows: A Poetic Quest

I realise that I've caused more harm than I've resolved,
With my twisted obligation to constantly get involved,
I had the ability to overwhelm even the mighty,
Into surrendering responsibilities, so that they'd like me.

Or so I thought, but it mainly had the opposite effect,
Yet any criticism of my actions, I'd just deflect,
My Daughter fled the country at 18, never to return,
And even when my Husband divorced me, I didn't learn.

Most things defining my life, seemed to slip away,
But my Son, Anthony didn't, I was glad that he stayed,
Although it meant I focused most of my attention on him,
At first he said nothing and simply took it on the chin.

Before long it got to him, back then I was clueless,
He hit the drink, the weed and lost his sense of humour,
Showing frustration; anxiety; plus flying off the handle,
Which I feel is my fault, as he followed my example.

In his younger years, before I got addicted to helping,
I had no way of concealing my issues, except shouting,
Being spiteful, playing mind-games, treating my kids poorly,
I thought they'd be happy I'd changed my ways, surely!?

My Husband and Daughter left, my Son stayed close by,
At first, I think he liked the convenience of me being docile,
Always saying yes, so afraid to tell him no,
Clutching to the belief that if I did, he too would go.

I used it as fuel to be the Mother I'd never been,
He called it the worst display of guilt he'd ever seen!
I must've opened old wounds, things worsened between us,
Plus he spent his life savings on drugs, in 3 months!

Once his money evaporated, he began stealing from me,
As I wouldn't support something so pointless and costly,
He stopped paying bills, I caved and paid them for him,
I had to get a second full-time job, just to afford it!

Confront The Shadows: A Poetic Quest

He got hold of lots of Cocaine, snorted a load,
Whilst driving, and ran over 2 people crossing the road,
Crashed into a lorry and lost both his legs,
I tried to be there for him, but he was a total mess!

After a tough month or so, he seemed to be coping,
But, considering what followed... more like, I was hoping!
He took a drug overdose and died in the bath,
I had a nervous breakdown, reunited with my past.

After 2 years of pills, care and therapy sessions,
I achieved a thoroughly cleansing, internal reflection,
The final stage of which, is this group bonding exercise,
To meet new people and begin to rebuild my life.

I no longer blame myself for my Son's suicide,
I tried to rectify his turmoil, but couldn't get inside,
I now help others again, but non-intrusively,
When you over-reach, it's bad for everyone, to some degree."

Heroless: (4) Hiroshima Times

Cocaine, opium and their derivatives,
Such as heroin, speedballs, freebase and crack,
Have a shrouded past, with silent witnesses,
Casualties and those with blood on their hands.

The victims suffer or die from a lack of awareness,
The guilty parties wish it would remain a mystery,
Though some might protect their ignorance, in all fairness,
Let's look at some interesting, unspoken history.

Opium was used by the ancient Egyptians,
The poppy features in their artwork 6000 years ago,
Used by Greeks and Romans, though mainly the minions,
Imported to China in 800 A.D, interesting to know.

Smoking opium was popular in China by the 1600's and,
Was transported by a Red Cross on a white shield,
Then in 1680 an English physician called Thomas Syndenham,
Developed *'uses'* for opiates in the medical field.

In 17th century Europe it *'treated'* many health issues,
Yet in 1729, the Chinese deemed its use illegal,
Followed by a ban on imports, not just its use,
Angering the British, who thrived on the demise of coloured people.

But demand for it remained, as many people were addicted,
So it was smuggled to them, supply was undeterred,
This caused the "Opium Wars" of 1839-60,
Until the smugglers had to take off, like the Thunderbirds.

Opium was given to soldiers as a *'treatment'*,
In the American Civil War of 1861-5,
'M*edicines*' not listing opiates as one of their ingredients,
It's amazing how long its *'miracle cure'* status survived!

Heroin was first produced in 1874 from it,
The Bayer Company sold it as a *'morphine substitution'*,
Growing concerns aside, it was also labelled a *'cough tonic'*!
The US Government then put a tax on opiate distribution.

Only to make it illegal to make or possess 10 years later,
But not before many were hooked, like anglers over-fishing,
Now, Coca is very ancient too and holds great danger,
Probably the most potent, risky stimulant of natural origin.

Used sparingly in ceremonies or climate survival pre-1532,
By Incas, Mayans and Indians, to gently stimulate,
But that all changed, when the Spanish invaded Peru,
'Forcing' its overuse, to help them control and manipulate.

A formula adopted swiftly in Europe's following crusades,
To conquer Asia, Africa, etc and leave them crawling,
Which is more cold and calculated than Saddam Hussein,
The West became more powerful, do you see a pattern forming?!

In 1855, Cocaine was synthesised from Coca leaves,
In 1880, psychologist Sigmund Freud (who used it himself),
Promoted the drug as a *'super tonic'*, as he believed,
It cured depression, impotence, plus other things as well.

In 1886, it gained more credibility as an ingredient,
In a new '*soft drink*' developed by John Pemberton,
Coca Cola's appeal was immense and immediate,
With both common folk and some Ladies and Gentlemen.

Due to this soft drink's stupendous accomplishment,
Cocaine and Opium laced elixirs, tonics and wines surfaced,
Many distinguished figures promoted them, including Thomas Edison,
But it was Hollywood's support, that excelled it the furthest.

Not far behind this was Freud's continued praises,
Prescribing Cocaine to his girlfriend, best friend and others,
He couldn't understand its effects or scientifically explain it,
His best effort was to call it a "*magical substance*"!

This only fuelled Cocaine's grasp on much of society,
Concern mounted, which led to a public outcry,
Forcing Coca Cola to withdraw its inclusion in 1903,
Only for snorting to become popular by 1905.

Within 5 years, there were frequent cases of nasal damage,
In hospitals and medical journals, the cause - Cocaine,
Septums falling out, like a grated cheese sandwich,
But certainly, the addicts weren't the only ones to blame.

In 1912 the United States Government announced,
5,000 Cocaine related deaths had occurred in one year,
More casualties and harm, could be seen the World around,
So why it took 8 more years to ban, simply it isn't clear!

This is much the same pace as was found with Opium,
However long you quiz, you'll receive no explanation,
Why something so obvious, could take so long,
Plus why the UK view the US as their *'role model'* nation.

Well, I can see a trend, I'm sure you will too,
The Eastern World, contains most of the Earth's natural wealth,
The best way for the West to possess this, voodoo,
Alter the East's mind-state, independence and health.

A nation's collective people, have the most potential power,
Most country's ruling powers feared this, few embraced it,
They ruled ferociously, so they wouldn't be devoured,
They used fear to keep control, yet sought a replacement.

Potent drugs were a great tool to weaken the masses,
To deviously take the wind out of their sails,
With no driving force, they would be left stranded,
And thus easily conquered, control would prevail.

High Society **2** – *The Rest Of Us* **Zilch**,
We've been murdered, oppressed, exploited, bamboozled,
The culprits hope we can't rise from the filth,
If *'procedure'* reigns, let's submit a refusal.

Reject their poison, ...voodoo ...virus,
We have the strength inside us, to block their interference,
They need our self-destruction, but we can be survivors,
Using awareness, positive change and perseverance!

Heroless: (5) Non-Organic Produce

Heading out into the September sun,
Sera made her way to the scheduled ceremony,
Knowing a new chapter in her life had begun,
Surrounded by friends, but still she felt empty.

Symphony Hall was massive, she finally found her spot,
Got comfortable and started watching the formalities,
After which, her fellow graduates got up and walked off,
Ready to be cheered on by companions and family.

When it was her turn, she wheeled herself around,
And waited in line to receive her certificate,
The butterflies intensified as it was announced,
"BSC, Pharmaceutical Science… Seraph Whitaker".

As she reached the other side with the scroll on her lap,
She gave a deep sigh, it was finally official,
A tear rolled down her cheek as she headed back,
She had no guests to wave at, purely her decision.

Confront The Shadows: A Poetic Quest

She'd bought 3 tickets, and it wasn't a no-show,
Merely a gesture, I know, not the simplest picture,
She didn't want anyone else to know,
They were for her deceased Mother, Father and Sister.

Sera wished they could be part of what she'd achieved,
By sheer determination, before the age of 21,
Already on the local Pharmaceutical Committee,
And had secured a Primary Care Pharmacist position.

Overcoming her so-called physical short-comings,
Mobility, genetic and general health issues,
The odds were against a positive person forming,
Especially with her Mother's suicide and drug abuse.

It's really been her whole life, not just today,
That the 3 empty spaces have remained vacant,
But she's still optimistic it will improve some day,
She'll build her own family and no longer be vagrant.

Yet everywhere she looked, the people that she saw,
Took most things for granted, without appreciating,
The fact that they had been blessed with it all,
Blind to the destruction they were swiftly creating.

Later in a nightclub, Sera thought to herself,
(It starts off with any excuse to get smashed,
Then it escalates, increasingly compromising their health,
Before they know it, some are hooked on Heroin or Crack!

Obviously there are those who escape its clutches,
But some do not, and it's them I'm worried for,
I don't want them to end up the way my Mum did,
And the millions of other victims, after and before.

Especially the children, they're the least aware,
Simply trying to be like their so called 'heroes',
And there are no big signs saying "**Danger!**" "**Beware!**"
Just "**Dya wanna be cool, or a total zero?!**"

Confront The Shadows: A Poetic Quest

Thus school kids as young as 8 are using Cocaine,
And 11 year olds upwards are using Heroin... madness!
The statistics collated for Class A usage in the UK,
Show there are more than 40,000 child Heroin addicts.

That's not including the adults, who should know better!
But denial of a problem is a common occurrence,
They'd be better off putting their limbs into a blender,
Than ignoring their issues and negative influence.

Thank goodness I was able to steer myself clear,
Of the hidden land-mines that most drugs represent,
I had to confront my obstacles, they didn't disappear,
Drugs might seem to get you high, but really secure descent.

I hope that users and potential ones, see the light,
And learn from our collective, reckless mistakes,
We could achieve so much, if we got our heads right,
The trap-door's not yet locked, I hope we escape!)

Pollen

If you look at the World through a convex lens,
You might see small particles more powerful than Samson,
That can cast spells on strangers and friends,
Causing a sudden, enchanting attraction.

What is this strong force? Where is it made?
How does it have such an affect on our functions?
Some call it hormones, energy, vibe, fate,
I call it pollen, as it's a natural conjunction.

The donor of the essence is known as the polleniser,
The pollinator transfers this to other folk,
Some flowers are self-fertile, this is often wiser,
Than relying on a medium for prosperity and growth.

Although most still rely on transport of some sort,
By either insects, birds, water or the wind,
Their future depends on them, there is no consort,
But as they give some out, they're usually pollinating.

Confront The Shadows: A Poetic Quest

The collection and drop off are at the same time,
At least they get something back, for sharing themselves,
They give bees their nectar too, which is kept in a hive,
But are eaten by the larvae, or put on sale on wide shelves.

Pollen can be harmful, it's not always a pro,
If someone's allergic, it can irritate them severely,
It depends on what type of essence is released though,
Positive, controlling, needy or fearing.

Positive is the best, it's contagious, refreshing,
Some flowers even imitate the pollinator's image,
Looking a certain way to secure more essence,
Is this cheating or merely survival of the fittest?

It's hard to say, but it brings me to my next topic,
About things thought to help your chance of pollination,
Such as nice clothes, fragrances, spontaneous antics,
A seductive smile, eye contact, a mutual acquaintance.

Great conversations, being sincerely considerate,
Humble, good morals, reputation, laughter,
Hygiene, grooming, being strong or sweet, diligence,
Confidence, focus and many more after.

The list could go on, but only helps so much,
Nothing's really certain, it's still a lottery,
Appreciate 3 numbers, the jackpot or just the bonus,
When you have good pollen, be sure to treat it properly.

Different types are attracted to different varieties,
There are many possibilities, some more fertile than others,
Good for one is not always good for others, it seems,
There's more to it, than what feels nice under the covers.

When I speak of pollen, I'm not merely mentioning sex,
But companionship, love, you know, the total package,
There's more to life than having a high pollen index,
Bonding with your soul-flower, will surely make you happy!

Confront The Shadows: A Poetic Quest

Rusty Cogs

Why does it have to be so gruelling,
To get my body to work today?
"Running on empty! In need of refuelling!"
Is the message that graces my vessel's display.

Nothing short of an uphill struggle,
Is what I'm experiencing at present,
Cringing as if I've just got in trouble,
And someone's determined to teach me a lesson.

I want to yell, "What have I done?!"
But fear this could lead to a harsher result,
I can't move a muscle, like I've been stunned,
Unable to fight it, but is this my fault?

Torn to pieces and stitched back together,
The plan was not followed on reassembly,
Not the first time though, I should've known better,
It's hard to maintain patience aplenty.

Confront The Shadows: A Poetic Quest

Something's once again under my skin,
Past my defences, well, nobody's perfect,
It commences its painful assault from within,
Aiming to see, who can push who the furthest.

Inside me it's bubbling, corroding my innards,
Like a bad tenant, it's hard to evict,
It heads inside further, mimicking splinters,
In this case, ignorance is clearly not bliss.

I have to confront my issues head-on,
They won't disappear, they'll only get worse,
If I let them be, so I need to get on,
By venting frustrations, you make them disperse.

Adjusting your outlook, you take control back,
Lubricating your system, so things aren't so bleak,
I tell you right now, I'd much rather have,
Tight cogs than popped clogs, any day of the week.

Exile Of A Scribbled Angel

I'm not where I used to, or long to be,
My home was the vast expanse of the Ocean,
I really miss its unique warmth and beauty,
But not the conflicting crosscurrent emotions.

Neither fearful, nor am I all that depressed,
Yet my exterior is both yellow and blue,
The Sea's turbulence made me overtly stressed,
That's when I knew, my exile was due.

Using the Sun and Moon as my allies,
I crossed over the inter-tidal zone,
To avoid being consumed, as many have tried,
Attempting to leave me, with nothing but bone.

Thankfully none of them finished me off,
Although I've a split lip, wounds and teeth marks,
Which has led to me frequently saying, "get lost!"
Preventing their hunt, being caught up and scarred.

Years have passed in this solitary dwelling,
The plan was never to remain here forever,
My heart's capacity is once again swelling,
And I hope one day soon, it will see brighter weather.

One thing's for sure, there'll be no more hooks,
Deceptive bait, or painful attachments,
Experienced by me, I'm now much more cautious,
No longer capricious or besotted with fragments.

It'll take sincere intentions and the use of a net,
Then gently placing me in a safe environment,
With nutritious sustenance, before I accept,
Stay put, show true happiness and become content.

It's a tall order, but far from impossible,
Anything less and I'll escape, like previous catches,
Me finding what I'm searching for, is certainly possible,
I'm ready and awaiting my total package.

Confront The Shadows: A Poetic Quest

Humble Crumble

It's astounding how long I remained single,
We're talking years, not months or weeks,
Inside I sensed I was hungry for love,
So I finally made the decision to eat.

An assortment of treats were all around me,
But nothing that would produce lasting flavour,
Please my connoisseur palate, leave my heart pounding,
I struggled to spot something I wanted to savour.

Analysing the situation with careful dissection,
Much in the vicinity would harm my health,
Convenience stores in every direction,
Instead, I chose to make something myself.

A specialist outlet caught my attention,
Membership followed, plus it's privileges,
An experience I enjoyed far beyond mention,
As I browsed potential matches, with my grocery list.

Confront The Shadows: A Poetic Quest

Avoiding processed, modified, unwholesome offerings,
Not wanting to compromise my well-being,
I was finally able to tick all the boxes,
Here come the butterflies and other warm feelings.

Finding the base ingredients of what I yearned for,
I outlined how I thought it would all come together,
Dedicating myself to a worthwhile cause,
Promising to nourish and prosper forever.

It's amazing how well this feast evolved,
Though more work was needed, before I could rate it,
Seeming unbelievable, like when magic's involved,
My mouth kept watering, I could almost taste it.

With time to spare until the oven was ready,
Some of the wait was filled with decorative effects,
I looked forward to putting this meal my belly,
But soon the dish's integrity, would be put to the test.

Unfortunately, its equilibrium was cryptically breached,
This once beautiful concoction, had become erratic,
Sadly, restoration could not be achieved,
It needed to be disposed of, like junk in the attic.

No cash here, no pay off, but also no regrets,
It fell apart, and though this is highly disappointing,
I'm conscious of my failure, but mainly feel blessed,
From glimpsing the bliss, I'll one day be enjoying.

The hunger pains have subsided at present,
I hope my appetite will recover soon,
While I utilise painful and endearing lessons,
To prevent starvation and impending amorous doom.

Yet quick-fixes and empty calories remain discouraged,
I'd still rather pursue a delicate mystery,
Those attaining rapture, often initially feel punished,
So I guess I'm destined to make culinary history!

Adiós!

What kind of World do we currently live in?
One where many remain so obtuse,
When presented with witty, enlightening lyrics,
They're increasingly viewed as a form of abuse.

The message is twisted beyond recognition,
The intended effect is turned on its head,
What happened to your once acute vision?
If the state is prevalent, discernment is dead!

Perhaps that comment has slender hyperbole,
There could be some other ill-logical reason,
Why you'd conspire, against kin who loved thee,
But my opinion is, it equates to treason!

You deluded yourself, then became so erratic,
Used mind games, nipping the hand that fed you,
Made me feel uneasy at home, like mice and maggots,
So it's no wonder, why I became such a rebel!

Confront The Shadows: A Poetic Quest

Even after all that, I might've been civil,
'Til you sped past the point of no return, sorry!
After brewing, you upgraded our conflict to physical,
Attacked me, then tried to choke the life out of me.

I freed my airway, and put out your raging furnace,
Shortly followed by calmly showing you the door,
With you and your stuff gone, I have to be earnest,
Things are much better, life's beautiful!

We'll never go back to the way we were,
You secured that verdict, with the way you've been,
I'm all for forgiveness, when it's rightly deserved,
But chances aren't tricks or treats at Halloween.

They're all used up now, spent rashly, squandered,
There was a lifetime supply, for someone decent,
Although, your true nature's that of a monster,
Beasts are not welcome, evolution's begun!

Forever Love

At a young age, my heart beat in a new way,
It found a new purpose... finding 'The One',
I knew I wouldn't get there that very day,
Yet it remained my major long-term goal.

Back then, I'd no clue what a quest I'd begun,
It would test me, with few encouraging signs,
I wanted to feel the embrace of the Sun,
But repeatedly felt love had closed all the blinds.

Most would give up, having felt what I'd felt,
And I'm not saying I didn't have several vacations,
But the ultimate aim, was to feel my heart melt,
Which in turn, meant pain and no room for sedation.

The journey was tough, the conditions extreme,
Though it wasn't all bad, at times I did smile,
Some people renewed my faith in the dream,
Prototypes to something I'd build in a while.

Confront The Shadows: A Poetic Quest

Tweaking the design, to eradicate flaws,
My patience persisted, my resolve held true,
Many years I stayed single, in aid of the cause,
And was rewarded ten-fold, when I finally found you!

My equations and theories, clicked right into place,
At the very moment our hearts and lips met,
Nothing beats your warmth, your smile or embrace,
You were so worth the wait, there can be no regret.

Every day's like my birthday, with you by my side,
Our love knows no bounds, it can't help but grow,
We're the happiest, we've both ever been in our lives,
Hence the fated, blessed union of Charming and Snow.

We've achieved so much, but we've barely begun,
We're such a great team, I can't ask for more,
I live, to make sure that you smile and feel loved,
Infinity-squared, is how much you're adored!

Confront The Shadows: A Poetic Quest

Pot Luck

We are all moving pieces on a large green vista,
There are dangers, in the far reaches of this plane,
Great holes to pluck you from view, a fate we are all due,
A factor of reality, that can't be dispelled in haste.

We're all in a game, in a multitude of colours,
Sharing many similarities, more than our differences,
When we interact, we help each other along our path,
Many options are on the table, we can collide or kiss.

But to get ahead, we have an established code to follow,
However, much is possible, with the right approach,
When our luck is spilled, we can feel racked with guilt,
If we act foul, our progress is stunted the most.

Still, the game rolls on regardless, fair play is rewarded,
Sometimes we miss opportunities, at times we get the lot,
So, before we're punked, snookered, or inevitably sunk,
Let's chalk it up to experience, and cue the next shot.

Empathy

Can you empathise with the strain that I feel?
Unabating pain taints my body and spirit,
The things that bind me, are far from ideal,
The burdens and stresses, I struggle to live with.

I'm known for my optimism and strength,
Good humour, patience and speaking politely,
Yet all of these attributes, seem almost spent,
And their revival seems to be fairly unlikely.

My body's worn out, my mind is depleted,
I'm running on vapours, not brimming with fuel,
How much longer can I go on, before I'm defeated,
Need rescuing, and mending with tools?

From a flawless possession to merely spare parts,
I've depreciated my personal worth's perception,
Weakened by the treadmill, too much for my heart,
But injury awaits, if I should change direction.

The future of my loved ones, keeps me fighting on,
Regardless of how much they value my efforts,
My surrender, will only make more things wrong,
Their happiness knows me as provider, protector.

I feel like I'm failing, though I'm giving my best,
My life is akin to a myth or dark fable,
It's like I'm being thoroughly put to the test,
To see if I'm worthy of becoming an Angel.

So I'm sorry if you feel I'm neglecting you some,
Overcoming these obstacles takes supreme focus,
If I need to, I'll keep trying 'til kingdom come,
To repel the grime, like the skin of a lotus.

On I go, through the snow, with toes cold as ice,
Not wanting to burden you with my harsh troubles,
Please don't look at me in a negative light,
Instead, shower me, with prayers and cuddles.

Blessed

What a turn of events, such a wacky reward,
For simply loving a lady with a beautiful soul,
It hadn't dawned on me, but thank you Lord,
For blessing me with a ready-made family to go.

Ultimately, I'd yearned to build my family unit,
But the right lady had never materialised,
If the foundations weren't right, no kids, like a eunuch,
Many times I was duped, but soon realised.

Thankfully, I was thorough in protecting my legacy,
So that I didn't get myself trapped in a lie,
Pledging my loyalty on such terms, lacks efficacy,
Being trapped in that swamp, a part of me would die.

Instead I found my best friend, my missing puzzle piece,
A strong bond from day one, magnetism, devotion,
The way we feel together, makes my whole life complete,
It's like we are both recipients of a love potion.

The bonus was becoming an instant Daddy of three,
To these beautiful seeds we can nurture together,
It truly melted my heart, the way they adopted me,
This is better than envisioned, may it last forever.

However, the Universe wasn't done imparting its gifts,
Fast forward to our Wedding day, our sacred matrimony,
Celibacy ended, our fourth child was conceived in bliss,
We awaited with excitement, as he grew inside his Mummy.

It's a shame this joyous pregnancy became so tough,
5 months in a wheelchair, with daily injections to boot,
The intense pain and hospital trips, were pretty rough,
Yet, it made his arrival all the more special, in truth.

Hence, we stand here as family, united, complete,
Yes, there are various frustrations, that's to be understood,
But how we found each other's beautifully unique,
Let's honour this blessing, by showering each other with love.

Confront The Shadows: A Poetic Quest

Meat The Muncher

I think I may well be addicted to meat,
Chicken, duck and succulent beef,
The flavours they conjure, my tongue's hypnotised,
Saliva starts flowing, when the meat slips inside.

I know some people will frown at this view,
Bear with me, while I evaluate what I chew,
I've made many changes in the interest of health,
But always after garnering the facts for myself.

I sat down, I researched, shocking things I did see,
And was blown away by a documentary called "Cowspiracy"
If you only take one thing from this poem, please watch it,
What you'll witness, will pop your eyes out of their sockets.

Some major problems, that this World is facing,
Can be linked to rearing livestock for food, frustrating,
So, why haven't environmental charities gone public,
With these disturbing facts, most appear ignorant of it.

When you dig a little deeper, the reasons become clear,
Those highlighting this issue, must overcome crippling fear,
Thousands of people were killed, for spreading the word,
Including a Nun in Brazil, shot in the head, absurd.

Howard Lyman spoke truths on The Oprah Winfrey Show,
Then spent 5 years and huge sums, defending his approach,
The power of the animal farming industry's incredible,
But regardless, here are some key facts to whet your whistle.

Livestock, especially cows, heavily impact global warming,
They're the top cause of low resources and forest culling,
One beefburger takes 3,000 litres of water to produce,
Or the equivalent of 2 months worth of showers, strewth!

850 Million people have no access to clean water,
11,000 litres makes only 1 pound of beef, your honour,
One third of the planet's water is used on animals we eat,
Over 40% of habitable land is used for this need.

Confront The Shadows: A Poetic Quest

Farming livestock is increasing, despite the adjunction,
It's responsible for 91% of the Amazon's destruction,
Without these trees and rainforests, humanity is doomed,
Yet, year on year, more animal foodstuffs are consumed.

1 in 9 people Worldwide, suffer from severe hunger,
But is producing meat, the way to tackle it, I wonder,
Looking at the figures, overall, it's very inefficient,
The growth hormones used, are harmful and stay with us.

This journey has been a real eye-opener for me,
Our blind hunger for meat and dairy, is a planetary disease,
We got here unknowingly, but we're now paying the price,
If we don't choose more wisely, humanity won't survive.

If we stop consuming animals, many issues will reverse,
We wield so much power, by redirecting our purse,
If you care for this World of ours, practice what you preach,
With what I've learnt, I can't continue munching the meat!

Killing My Buzz

My whole buzzing World has began to crumble,
I'm an endangered species, like tigers in the jungle,
Oh, how rude of me, hello, my name is Bumble,
Our survival's beeing threatened, of course, I'm disgruntled.

My kind have thrived for millions of years in the wild,
With little change in all that time, to our culture or hives,
Everybeedy knows their roles, their completion is precise,
So, why all of a sudden, do we feel the end is nigh?!

The first issue is that for millenia, we've been oppressed,
Our honey has been stolen, to serve the needs of men.
We lack the natural food that's made to give us strength,
Our babies become malnourished, our energy is spent.

Some of us are kept in man-made hives, it'd be okay,
But we're put to sleep, and again they take our food away,
Imprisoned in a system that we didn't want or make,
Trillions of us have died, beeing nothing but a slave.

Confront The Shadows: A Poetic Quest

Our global numbers are declining, demands on us increase,
Not beeing cared for properly, we are now prone to disease,
Mites, parasites and other factors, bringing us to our knees,
  CCD is more deadly than facing a fire breathing beast.

  Intensive human farming, has meant habitat destruction,
    No biodiversity, we struggle to perform basic functions,
Pesticides attack our nervous system, ending our gumption.
Greatly affecting our sensitive navigation and reproduction.

    Did you know, we pollinate more than a third,
    Of the entire World's food supply? ...that's my word,
  We keep plants and crops alive, yet are treated like turd,
I had a dream last night, we finally got what we deserved.

But there is no delegate for us, no Martin Luther Sting,
  No way to express the hardships we're experiencing,
  Like 97% of our wild-flower meadows disappearing,
In the last 70 years, because of man, it's really depressing.

Any one of these issues is damaging to beekind,
And I can't do justice to their impact when combined,
Its a miracle that up to now, we've actually survived,
But we're nearing an extinction event that won't rewind.

Us pollinators don't have long, before we're wiped out,
Which will scar the planet, making global survival go south,
Plus destroy most things you like to put into your mouth,
Death will be more common, sporadic famine and drought.

No local produce, you'll have to eat things made in a lab,
Those companies will have a choke hold on your life, fact,
To avoid this future, quickly change the way that you act,
If you sit back and do nothing, soon enough, you'll feel bad.

Mankind'll join my ancestors, if this plea's not heeded.
Sustainable agriculture and true animal welfare's needed,
Reduce pesticides and pollution, greed must be seceded,
Buy organic, and make places bee friendly, we all need it.

The Difference

Some cannot see it, the traits are a blur,
Some damn them all, having been badly hurt,
Pain clouds their judgement, they can't measure worth,
All rejected, without so much as a word.

However, there are stark differences to be had,
Should individuals on their own honour stand,
If the deeds and heart are the yardstick of rank,
You'll see differences between a male and a man.

A male's full of ego, bravado and such,
Testosterone overload, in a ploy to be butch,
Showing no signs of weakness, Vegas or bust,
Gambling with relationships, squandering trust.

A man seems more timid, less in your face,
He has less to prove, moving at his own pace,
More secure in himself, less filled with hate,
More loving, considerate, and open to change.

Males ignore character, valuing masks,
Using tricks and taunts; mind games; attacks,
Showing strong facades, but are weaker than wax,
Hypnotising those close to them, which never lasts.

Men are peaceful; nurturing; empathetic; kind;
Don't make a scene, they lead with their mind,
Think things through patiently, taking their time,
They're loyal, trustworthy, bubbly, refined.

A male has a tendency to think with his groin,
He's lustful; inappropriate; vulgar and spoilt,
Manipulates, abuses, plays with feelings like toys,
A real piece of work, that you're wise to avoid.

A man is a healer, protector, provider,
Gives his all for his loved ones, lifts them higher,
He's a role model, who can truly inspire,
Removes danger, shields hearts from the fire.

Confront The Shadows: A Poetic Quest

Males may be more popular in society,
Some have high paying jobs, ride in limousines,
They like living in a World full of greed,
They take what they want, but lack what they need.

A man deserves much more respect than he gets,
But he rarely complains, busy giving his best,
In a worthwhile cause, he'll gladly invest,
If you have a man on your team, you're blessed.

Yet, I feel it's only right to remind you all,
Nobody's perfect, even an angel can fall,
A man should be praised for his efforts overall,
A hiccup, shouldn't mean your respect's reversal.

Male's are complex, no matter the genus,
Men are from Mars, women from Venus,
Not all guys are ruled by their penis,
I hope this mends some of the bridges between us.

I Knows It, I Grows It

I'd like to take a moment, to honour a hero of mine,
A man who had a huge and special impact on my life,
He was taken from us, but his deeds can be discovered,
In this celebration of the late, great Eglon Ruddock.

Born and raised in Jamaica, this young boy was no fool,
He walked for several miles each day, just to get to school,
Though he didn't go for long, he still keenly fed his head,
Learning useful things from his Mum and Dad instead.

In 1955, he came to England, a 21 day journey,
Pricey for a 30 year old, £4000 in today's money,
On arrival, he nearly turned back, it was cold and he said,
"What a place, the trees no even 'ave leaves 'pon dem!"

Once settled, he sent for the love of his life, Beaulah,
Who came over, to help their dreams come true together,
They married, built a happy home and had a big family,
Even with these obligations, they exuded love and charity.

Eglon taught his kids and grandkids, songs and counting,
He also saved a boy in the River Thames from drowning,
Jumping in, without knowing if he could swim himself,
Thank fully, he could enough, to get the two of them out.

Eglon was as good at cooking, as he was generous,
So, it's safe to say, there were never any leftovers,
He helped his neighbours, and sent money back'a yard,
Aiding his family in Jamaica, thanks to working very hard.

His work ethic, was inspiring, his radiance, almost blinding,
He had a great sense of humour, and hysterical timing,
A great person to be around, exceptional company,
Never a dull moment, laughing, learning, discovery.

He was undisputed champion in draughts and dominoes,
When playing him, I swear he knew the tactics you'd chose,
Hearing, "2 moves an' you finish'!" You'd show strength,
He'd say, "Oh, you gonna fight?! A'right t'ree moves den!"

Confront The Shadows: A Poetic Quest

It was like something straight from a martial arts movie,
He was Sam Seed, us? Jackie Chan the newbie,
"Mek me tell you somet'in...", cue truths about the World,
When we used this wisdom, opportunities unfurled.

Eglon treated his kid's friends, like family members,
He also loved church, memorising many a bible verse,
His faith was contagious, not just the spiritual kind,
His faith in others was inspiring, it even strengthened mine.

He loved others like himself, was humble and respectful,
When he left us, he merely slipped into the next room,
We still feel his presence, his influence and love,
I'm sure he's building us a home, in the stars above.

"I knows it, I grows it, like Jamaican ginger",
Another of your sayings, that will forever linger,
Your legacy lives on, inspiring the masses,
"We'll see you again, my friend, when we get our glasses."

Confront The Shadows: A Poetic Quest

The Age Of Plenty

I love this World with all my heart, but does it loves me?
The driving force in use today, is a manifestation of greed,
We're all so focused on what we want, others are forgotten,
If this selfish culture's accepted, our insides become rotten.

I see such beauty here and there, yet I yearn for better,
I'd love it if we cared so much, it brought us all together,
If those with the most riches, simply squander and waste,
We should not feed their habit, but intervene with haste.

We need to act efficiently, in the way we deal with poverty,
Only supporting causes, who use their funding properly,
No banquets, contracts, costly managers, up to little good,
But ones who greatly help the needy, as they rightly should.

When I've satisfied my needs, the excess is not for wants,
I'm blessed with this abundance, for a generous response,
To care for neighbours far and wide, as I do my family,
Hunger and needless suffering will cease, if we do this happily.

Dearly Departed

I haven't moved on, I'm covered in moss,
You weren't a possession, but I still feel the loss,
My wounds feel as fresh, as when this pain started,
The moment you became my dearly departed.

Part of me wishes I'd gone in your place,
You meant so much to us, it seems such a waste,
Although, this is seemingly selfish of me,
As you'd be in mourning, with *your* loved one deceased.

Ignore me, it's just harsh inside, feeling like this,
When you passed away, you left a huge deficit,
In my heart; my life; my arms; and my smile,
What I'd give, to once more feel your warmth for a while!

Your wisdom and insight, your humour and love,
Gifts I only now realise the true value of,
Compassion; acceptance; humility; grace,
The traits that you showed in a million ways.

Confront The Shadows: A Poetic Quest

The day that you left us, the World took a blow,
Was left bruised and confused, and tears they did flow,
But most fail to grasp its total significance,
A fallen Angel, given their well earned deliverance.

You weren't perfect, but your efforts should be applauded,
Probably a key reason why your level-up was awarded,
You graduated to a higher plane of existence,
I know you're in a better place, despite my resistance.

I feel you had more to do here, before your transition,
But guess you've been chosen for a more crucial mission,
So I'll carry your baton, and finish your event,
Time spent expanding your legacy, is time well spent.

You're an inspiration to me, that's an understated fact,
The weight of my love for you, could make a diamond crack,
Our connection is deep rooted, like that of the elm,
We'll reunite some day, in your new enchanted realm.

About The Author

Hello, I'm Following Whispers, an English poet and author who has been writing poetry for over two decades. I was initially inspired to put pen to paper after a series of difficult events that shook me to the core, which left me struggling to make sense of what had happened and why; make sense of the somewhat merciless world around me; my emotions; who I was; and more importantly, who I wanted to become.

I am a self-confessed Geek who can get deep sometimes (as I have done for most of this book), but I generally don't take myself too seriously, I just love to have fun, inspire myself and others, plus be inspired by the things and people around me, something you'll see much more of in my future poetry book releases.

In my early twenties, I realised that beauty could be born out of not only love, but also pain and other motivations. The more I used this therapeutic implement, the more I realised that it helped me to find a silver lining in even the darkest emotions, experiences, observations and topics; find positivity even in the face of extreme negativity; find strength when I was being forced to feel weak; and find hope that my tomorrows would be brighter.

If you want to read my new poetry offerings for free, please visit **followingwhispers.com** where you'll find my blog (free email subscription available), plus details about my other books and my social media links, so that you can follow me, connect with me and spark up a conversation.

I would also absolutely love it if you left me a book review on the online listing for this title, be it on Amazon, Kobo, or any website or app that represents the place where you purchased my book. If this book was acquired from me directly, anywhere you can find it online will suffice. Thank you so much for your support, it helps me more than you could ever imagine, so thank you for showing some love!

www.ingramcontent.com/pod-product-compliance
Lightning Source LLC
Chambersburg PA
CBHW071022080526
44587CB00015B/2455